MW01171333

Dedication

A Taste of Southern Soul: Recipes That Feed The Soul has truly been a pleasure to create and is a genuine labor of love. Featuring a vast collection of delicious recipes, including desserts, cocktails/mocktails, and table desserts, A Taste of Southern Soul is sure to satisfy your sweet tooth and bring a taste of Southern soul to your kitchen. Enjoy!

Dedicated to my favorite girls:
MOM, RENA, BIG MAMA, & LUCILLE

Foreword

Writing this foreword for our dear friend Jeromie "Kake King" Jones' latest cookbook, A Taste of Southern Soul, is an honor that fills us with immense pride and joy. "Family like no other," indeed. From the very beginning, our relationship with Jeromie has been built on unwavering support and genuine authenticity. From our first meeting, there was something about him that felt familiar, comfortable, and sincere—he felt like family. The title of our group chat, "Family Like No Other," couldn't be more fitting, as we have shared life's ups and downs together over the years.

From the start, we recognized his uniqueness. His outgoing personality and extraordinary drive and ambition set him apart. We were certain that his unapologetic and steadfast commitment to staying true to himself would take him further than even he could imagine. From pop up shops and luncheons on Sundays to the most important days of our lives, Jeromie wasn't just there—he was a huge presence, showing up in ways we could never repay.

Our journey has been as rich and flavorful as the recipes you will discover within these pages. As two of his closest friends, we've witnessed firsthand the passion and dedication that Jeromie pours into his craft, and this cookbook is a testament to that devotion. Even from hundreds of miles away, the images of those perfectly plated Sunday meals shared on social media make our mouths water.

Jeromie's culinary journey began in his home kitchen, where he experimented with traditional desserts that we all know and love, to Southern recipes handed down through generations. In true Jeromie fashion, he always added something extra that set him apart from the rest. Over the years, we've been fortunate to taste the evolution of his creations—each one a perfect blend of tradition and innovation, always prepared with love and a touch of his unique flair. His dishes are more than just food; they are a celebration of Southern culture, community, and the comforting embrace of home.

Foreword

In A Taste of Southern Soul, Jeromie invites you into his world, offering a collection of recipes that are both heartfelt and deeply rooted in his Southern heritage. From savory classics to sweet indulgences, every recipe reflects his journey from a passionate home baker to a celebrated culinary artist and business owner. He has candidly shared with his followers and "cake cousins" both his triumphs and his setbacks in crafting his vision of the perfect recipe compilation, further highlighting the genuineness of his culinary journey. His commitment and enthusiasm for educating others, even at the expense of disclosing his own mistakes, are qualities worthy of admiration and respect.

Jeromie's story is one of resilience and creativity. His path wasn't always easy, but his determination to bring joy through his food never wavered. We've seen him turn moments of adversity into opportunities for growth, all while maintaining a spirit of generosity and kindness that defines him. This cookbook goes beyond being merely a collection of dishes; it's a narrative of his life, filled with the vibrant essence of Southern hospitality.

As you embark on your own culinary adventures with this cookbook, we hope you feel the same warmth and inspiration that we do whenever we share a meal with Jeromie. His recipes are crafted to bring people together, to create moments of connection and joy.

So, gather your loved ones, roll up your sleeves, and dive into the delicious world of A Taste of Southern Soul.

With heartfelt appreciation and excitement,

RENISHA AND CHANDRA

A
TASTE
OF
Southern
SOUL

Recipes That Feed the Soul

Contents

MEASUREMENTS
&
Flavor
PAIRINGS

Measurements

Essential Kitchen Conversions

Dry Conversions & Equivalents

3 teaspoons = 1 Tablespoon = 1/16 cup

6 teaspoons = 2 Tablespoons = 1/8 cup

12 teaspoons = 4 Tablespoons = 1/ 4 cup

24 teaspoons = 8 Tablespoons = 1/2 cup

36 teaspoons = 12 Tablespoons = 3/4 cup

48 teaspoons = 16 Tablespoons = 1 cup

Weight

1 gram = 0.35 ounces

100 grams = 3.5 ounces

500 grams = 1.1. pounds

1 kilogram = 35 ounces

Liquid Conversions & Equivalents

8 fluid ounces = 1 cup - 1/2 pint = 1/4 quart

16 fluid ounces = 2 cups - 1 pint = 1/2 quart

32 fluid ounces = 4 cups = 2 pints = 1 quart = 1/4 gallon

128 fluid ounces = 16 cups = 8 pints = 4 quarts = 1 gallon

1 Cup Equivalents

1 cup = 8 fluid ounces

1 cup = 16 Tablespoons

1 cup = 48 teaspoons

1 cup = 1/2 pint

1 cup = 1/4 quart

1 cup = 1/16 gallon

1 cup = 240 ml

Butter

1 cup butter = 2 sticks = 8 ounces = 230 grams = 8 Tablespoons

U.S. to Metric Baking Conversions

1/5 teaspoon = 1 ml

1 teaspoon = 5 ml

1 Tablespoon = 15 ml

1 fluid ounce = 30 ml

1 cup = 237 ml

1 pint (2 cups) = 473 ml

1 quart (4 cups) = .95 liter

1 gallon (16 cups) = 3.8 liters

1 ounce = 28 grams

1 pound = 454 grams

Measurements

Baking Pan Conversions

	Pan size	Volume
Round	8 x 2 inches	6 cups
	9 x 2 inches	8 cups
	10 x 2 inches	11 cups
Springform	9 x 2 inches	10 cups
	9 x 3 inches	12 cups
	10 x 2.5 inches	12 cups
Bundt	7.5 x 3 inches	6 cups
	9 x 3 inches	9 cups
	10 x 3.5 inches	12 cups
Square	8 x 8 x 1.5 inches	6 cups
	8 x 8 x 2 inches	8 cups
	9 x 9 x 1.5 inches	8 cups
Rectangle	11 x 17 x 2 inches	10 cups
	13 x 9 x 2 inches	14 cups
Loaf	8 x 4 x 2.5 inches	4 cups
	8.5 x 4.5 x 2.5 inches	6 cups
	8.5 x 4.5 x 2.5 inches	8 cups
Heart	8 x 2.5 inches	8 cups

Essential Baking Conversions

1 cup all-purpose flour $=$ 4.5 ounces

1 cup rolled oats $=$ 3 ounces

1 large egg $=$ 1.7 ounces

1 cup butter $=$ 8 ounces

1 cup milk $=$ 8 ounces

1 cup heavy cream $=$ 8.4 ounces

1 cup granulated sugar $=$ 7.1 ounces

1 cup packed brown sugar $=$ 7.75 ounces

1 cup vegetable oil $=$ 7.7 ounces

1 cup unsifted powdered sugar $=$ 4.4 ounces

Essential Baking Supplies

Scan Here

Flavor Pairings

In the world of baking and cooking, vanilla stands as a timeless and versatile flavor enhancer. Its subtle sweetness and delicate aroma elevate both sweet and savory dishes alike. Whether infused into custards, cakes, or even savory sauces, vanilla adds a comforting depth that balances and rounds out other flavors.

Citrus, on the other hand, brings a bright and zesty dimension to recipes, offering a burst of freshness and acidity. Lemon, lime, and orange zest or juice can uplift desserts like tarts, cakes, and sorbets, as well as savory dishes such as marinades, dressings, and seafood.

Fruits and berries offer a spectrum of flavors, from the tartness of cranberries to the sweetness of ripe strawberries. Their natural sugars can complement richer ingredients in baked goods, while also bringing vibrant color and texture to salads, sauces, and even savory glazes for meats.

Spices, with their aromatic and warming qualities, add depth and complexity to dishes. Cinnamon, nutmeg, ginger, and cloves infuse desserts with comforting warmth, while savory spices like cumin, coriander, and paprika lend depth to meats, stews, and curries.

Ultimately, there is no right or wrong way to pair flavors in cooking and baking. Experimentation is key, as blending unexpected combinations can yield delightful and innovative results. So, let your taste buds guide you, and don't hesitate to embark on culinary adventures to discover new and exciting flavor pairings.

Things to pair with	Fruit & Berries	Spices & Herbs	Nuts	Chocolate & Caramel
Lemon	raspberry, blueberry, black currant, blackberry red currant, strawberry, orange, passion fruit, plum, cherry, apple, rhubarb	vanilla, cardamom, seed, thyme, rosemary, basil, aniseed, fennel seed	almond, pistachio	white chocolate, caramel
Orange	apple, blackberry, lemon, grapefruit, pear, apricot	cardamom, vanilla, cinnamon, nutmeg, ginger, star anise, basil, mint	hazelnut, almond, pecan, pistachio, peanut, coconut	dark chocolate, milk chocolate, white chocolate, caramel
Lime	strawberry, pineapple, apple, kiwi, mango, orange, grapefruit	cardamom, ginger, vanilla, clove, star anise, thyme, basil, mint, chili	hazelnut, pecan coconut	dark chocolate, white chocolate, caramel
Apple	blackberry, black currant, plum, citrus, cranberry, apricot	cinnamon, cardamom, ginger, vanilla, clove, anise, tarragon	almond, hazelnut, walnut	milk chocolate, caramel
Pear	blackberry plum, citrus, raspberry	vanilla, ginger, cardamom, nutmeg	almond, hazelnut, pecan, peanut	dark chocolate, milk chocolate, white chocolate, caramel
Passion fruit	kiwi, mango, orange, pineapple, strawberry, lemon, lime	vanilla, ginger, cardamom, chili	almond, hazelnut, pistachio, coconut, peanut	dark chocolate, milk chocolate, white chocolate, caramel
Cherry	lemon, orange, plum	vanilla, ginger, cardamom, fennel	almond, hazelnut, coconut	dark chocolate, white chocolate, caramel
Mango	lemon, orange, kiwi, raspberry, strawberry, pineapple, pomegranate	vanilla, ginger, cardamom, chili, nutmeg, mint, basil	almond, cashew, pistachio, coconut, hazelnut	dark chocolate, white chocolate
Raspberry	lemon, lime, mango, orange, pear, rhubarb	vanilla, cinnamon, fennel, star anise, tarragon, thyme, mint	almond, pistachio, pecan, coconut	dark chocolate, white chocolate

POUND CAKES & BUNDT CAKES

COTTON CANDY CREAM CHEESE POUND CAKE

- 3 sticks unsalted butter, softened to room temperature
- 8 oz. full-fat cream cheese, softened to room temperature
- 3 cups granulated sugar
- 1/3 cup sour cream, at room temperature
- 1 tsp. pure vanilla extract
- 2 tsp. cotton candy extract
- 1 tsp. strawberry extract
- 6 large eggs, at room temperature
- 3 cups cake flour (spooned & leveled)
- 1/2 tsp. baking powder
- 1/8 tsp. salt
- 3 - 4 gel colors of your choice

INSTRUCTIONS

1. Beat eggs into mixture one at a time on low speed. Avoid over-mixing.
2. After adding the 6th egg, stop mixer and add cake flour, baking powder, and salt. Mix on medium speed until just combined. Use spatula to ensure no lumps remain. Batter will be thick and creamy.
3. Divide batter by color. Gently fold in gel colors until just combined.
4. Evenly pour batter into prepared pan. Tap pan on counter to remove air bubbles.
5. Bake at 325°F for 1 hour 20 minutes. Use toothpick to check doneness.
6. Allow cake to cool for 2-3 minutes, then invert onto wire rack. Brush with simple syrup for added moisture. Cool completely before glazing.
7. Prepare glaze.

MRS. B'S
NANA PUDDING CAKE

INGREDIENTS

- 1 box yellow cake mix
- 1 cup all-purpose flour sifted
- 1 cup granulated sugar
- 1 box banana cream pudding mix
- 2 tsp. pure vanilla extract
- 2 Tbsp. banana extract
- 4 large eggs, at room temperature
- 1/2 cup vegetable oil or 1 stick of unsalted butter
- 1 cup water
- 1/2 cup buttermilk
- 1 banana blended with 1 tsp. lemon juice
- 2 cups vanilla wafers

FILLING

- 1 block cream cheese
- 1 cup confectioners' sugar
- 5-6 Tbsp. heavy cream
- 2 tsp. banana extract
- 1 tsp. vanilla extract or vanilla bean paste
- 1 tablespoon sweetened condensed milk

GLAZE

- 1 cup powder sugar
- 3/4 cup heavy cream (more depending on the consistency you would like.)
- 1-2 drops yellow food coloring
- 1 tsp. vanilla extract
- 2 tsp. banana extract

INSTRUCTIONS

1. Preheat oven to 325°F. Generously grease a 10-12 cup Bundt pan with butter or nonstick spray.
2. Using a handheld or stand mixer fitted with a paddle or whisk attachment, add all dry ingredients to bowl and whisk.
3. Add in wet water, buttermilk, eggs, oil, flavoring.
4. Mix all ingredients until combined.
5. Once mixed, fold in blended bananas.
6. Crush 1 cup of wafers and add to the bottom of the pan.
7. Pour batter into pan and tap on counter to release any air bubbles.
8. Bake at 325°F for 40-50 minutes or until toothpick comes out clean.
9. Once baked flip cake onto wire rack and allow to cool.
10. While cake is cooling prepare the glaze.

Optional: Drizzle cake with white chocolate

COOKIES & CREAM BUNDT CAKE

INGREDIENTS

For the Cake:
- 1 box white cake mix
- 1 cup all-purpose flour, sifted
- 1 cup sugar
- 1 box Oreo Cookies & Cream gelatin pudding mix
- 3 eggs
- 1 cup water
- 1/2 cup buttermilk
- 1/2 cup vegetable oil
- 1 tsp. almond extract
- 1 Tbsp. vanilla extract
- 1 cup crushed Oreo cookies

For Preparing the Pan:
1/2 cup crushed Oreo cookies

INSTRUCTIONS

1. Preheat the oven to 325°F.
2. Grease and flour a cake pan, then sprinkle 1/2 cup of crushed Oreo cookies on the bottom. Set aside.
3. In a large bowl, combine white cake mix, sifted flour, sugar, and Oreo Cookies & Cream gelatin pudding mix. Add eggs, water, buttermilk, vegetable oil, almond extract, and vanilla extract. Mix on low speed, then on medium for 2 minutes until smooth.
4. Fold in crushed Oreo cookies. Pour the batter into the prepared pan, spreading evenly. Tap the pan to remove air bubbles.
5. Bake for 40-50 minutes, or until a toothpick comes out clean. Let the cake cool in the pan for 10 minutes, then transfer to a wire rack to cool completely.
6. Once cooled, frost with your desired frosting and decorate with additional crushed Oreos if desired. Slice and serve.

You can also add a layer of frosting between two cake layers for a layered cake, or make cupcakes using the same batter and adjust the baking time accordingly.

OLD FASHIONED
LEMON POUND CAKE

INGREDIENTS

- 3 cups cake flour
- 1/2 tsp. baking soda
- 1 1/2 cups unsalted butter, at room temperature
- 3 cups granulated sugar
- zest of two lemons
- 6 large eggs, at room temperature
- 1 tsp. lemon extract
- 1/2 tsp. vanilla extract
- 1/2 cup evaporated milk
- 1/2 cup sour cream
- 1/2 cup heavy cream
- Juice of one lemon

SIMPLE SYRUP

- For the Simple Syrup:
- 1/2 cup white sugar
- 1/2 cup water
- juice of one lemon

GLAZE

- 1 cup powdered sugar
- Juice of 1/2 a lemon
- 2 Tbsp. milk
- 1tsp. vanilla extract

INSTRUCTIONS

1. **Do not preheat the oven.** Place the cake in a cold oven, set to 325°F, and bake for 1 hour 15 minutes or until a toothpick comes out clean.
2. Whisk cake flour and baking soda. Set aside.
3. Cream butter, sugar, and lemon zest until light and fluffy (6-7 minutes). Add eggs one at a time, beating well after each. Mix in lemon and vanilla extracts.
4. Gradually add flour mixture, alternating with evaporated milk, sour cream, and heavy cream. Stir in lemon juice.
5. Pour batter into the prepared pan, smooth the top, and place in the oven.
6. Prepare simple syrup by boiling sugar, water, and lemon juice until sugar dissolves. Remove from heat.
7. Pour syrup over hot cake. Cool in the pan for 15 minutes, then invert onto a wire rack. Glaze with powdered sugar, milk, vanilla, and lemon juice.

STRAWBERRY CREAM CHEESE POUND CAKE

INGREDIENTS

- 1 and 1/2 cups unsalted butter, softened to room temperature
- 8 oz. full-fat brick cream cheese, softened to room temperature
- 2 and 1/2 cups granulated sugar
- 1/3 cup sour cream, at room temperature
- 2 tsp. pure vanilla bean gel
- 1 Tbsp. strawberry extract
- 6 large eggs, at room temperature
- 3 cups cake flour (spooned & leveled)
- 1/2 tsp. baking powder
- 1/8 tsp. salt
- 1 cup freeze dried strawberries

INSTRUCTIONS

1. Preheat oven to 325°F.
2. Generously grease a 10-12 cup Bundt pan with butter or nonstick spray.
3. Using a handheld or stand mixer, beat butter until smooth.
4. Add cream cheese, sugar, sour cream, and vanilla; beat until creamy.
5. Add eggs one at a time, then mix in cake flour, freeze-dried strawberries, baking powder, and salt until just combined. Ensure smooth batter; fold in additional freeze-dried strawberries.
6. Pour into pan; bake for 75-95 minutes, tenting with foil halfway through. Test with toothpick. Invert and cool on wire rack.
7. Store leftover cake in an airtight container.

My Big Mama's Favorite Pound Cake!
Cream Cheese Pound Cake

INGREDIENTS

- 3 sticks unsalted butter, softened to room temperature
- 8 oz. full-fat cream cheese, softened to room temperature
- 3 cups granulated sugar
- 1/3 cup sour cream, at room temperature
- 2 tsp. pure vanilla extract
- 1 tsp. pure almond extract
- 1 tsp. butter extract
- 6 large eggs, at room temperature
- 3 cups cake flour (spooned & leveled)
- 1/2 tsp. baking powder
- 1/8 tsp. salt

INSTRUCTIONS

1. Generously grease a 10-12 cup Bundt pan with butter or nonstick spray.
2. Using a handheld or stand mixer, beat butter until smooth, about 1 minute; scrape down sides.
3. Add cream cheese and beat until smooth.
4. Add sugar, sour cream, and vanilla; beat until creamy; scrape down sides.
5. On low speed, add eggs 1 at a time, stopping after the 6th egg.
6. Add flour, baking powder, and salt; mix on medium speed just until combined. Ensure smooth batter with no lumps at the bottom of the bowl.
7. Pour batter into pan, tapping to remove bubbles.
8. Bake at 325°F for 1 hour 20 minutes; test with toothpick.
9. Invert onto wire rack to cool completely.

CLASSIC VANILLA POUND CAKE

INGREDIENTS

- 1-1/2 cups (3 sticks) unsalted butter, softened
- 3 cups granulated sugar
- 6 large eggs
- 3 cups all-purpose flour
- 1 cup whole milk
- 1 Tbsp. pure vanilla extract
- 1/2 tsp. salt

INSTRUCTIONS

1. Your oven does not need to be preheated, once all ingredients are mixed, place cake into cold oven and set temperature to 325°F.
2. In a large mixing bowl, cream together the softened butter and granulated sugar until light and fluffy.
3. Add the eggs, one at a time, beating well after each addition.
4. Gradually add the flour to the butter mixture, alternating with the milk. Begin and end with the flour mixture. Mix until just combined.
5. Stir in the vanilla extract and salt, ensuring they are evenly distributed throughout the batter.
6. Pour the batter into the greased pan and smooth the top with a spatula.
7. Bake in the preheated oven for one hour and twenty minutes, or until a toothpick inserted into the center comes out clean.
8. Allow the cake to cool in the pan for about 5 minutes, then transfer it to a wire rack to cool completely.

This recipe yields a moist and buttery pound cake with a delightful vanilla flavor. It's a versatile cake that can be enjoyed on its own or paired with fresh berries, whipped cream, or a simple vanilla glaze using the recipe in the **Glazes, Frostings & Fillings section.**

PECAN UPSIDE DOWN BUNDT CAKE

INGREDIENTS

Cake Batter
- 1 box vanilla cake mix
- 3 large eggs
- 1/2 cup vegetable oil
- 1 cup water
- 3 Tbsp. sour cream

Pecan Topping
- 1/2 cup butter (melted)
- 1/2 cup brown sugar (packed)
- 1/4 cup corn syrup
- 1/4 tsp. salt
- 1 cup chopped pecans

INSTRUCTIONS

Preheat oven to 350°F. Prepare your bundt pan by liberally spraying it with nonstick spray and set aside.

Pecan Topping
1. Combine melted butter, brown sugar, corn syrup and salt into a medium bowl and whisk until the brown sugar is slightly dissolved.
2. Add pecans and stir until combined. Pour into the bottom of prepared bundt pan and set aside.

Cake Batter
1. Combine cake mix, eggs, vegetable oil, water, and sour cream in a large bowl and mix according to package directions. Pour batter into prepared pan and on top of the pecan topping. Be sure to spread it into an even layer.
2. Bake in a 350°F oven for 40-45 minutes or until a toothpick inserted into the center of the cake comes out clean.
3. Remove from oven and place onto a cooling rack for 10 minutes. After 10 minutes run a knife around the edges of the cake. Then invert your Pecan Upside Down Bundt Cake onto a cake plate and cool completely. If pecans stick to the bottom of the pan just use your fingers to remove them and place them onto the cake.
4. Store your Pecan Upside Down Bundt Cake at room temperature or in the refrigerator for up to 3 days.

6 FLAVOR POUND CAKE

INGREDIENTS

- 3 cups cake flour
- 1 tsp. baking powder
- 3 cups sugar
- 3 sticks butter
- 1/2 cups butter-flavored shortening
- 5 large eggs
- 1 cup milk alternate starting with flour
- 1 tsp. of 6 flavors. I used almond, butter, vanilla, rum, lemon, coconut.

Glaze
- 2 cups powdered sugar
- 1/2 cup milk
- 1 tsp. of any of the 6 flavors used in the cake.

I used almond, butter, vanilla, rum, lemon, and coconut.

Simple Syrup
- Equal parts sugar and water.
- I added almond extract to flavor the syrup. I like to spritz or brush cakes with syrup to give them a sheen.

INSTRUCTIONS

1. Bake at 325°F for 1 hour 15 minutes. Times may vary due to different ovens, but check after 1 hour and 5 minutes through the oven window. You can pretty much see if a cake is ready for you to open the door so that you can check with a toothpick.
2. Allow the cake to cool in the pan for about 5 minutes, then transfer it to a wire rack to cool completely.

KEY LIME
CREAM CHEESE POUND CAKE

INGREDIENTS

- 3 sticks (1 1/2 cups) unsalted butter
- 3 cups granulated sugar
- 3 cups all-purpose flour
- 8 oz. cream cheese
- 1/2 tsp. baking powder
- 1/2 tsp. baking soda
- 6 extra large eggs
- 1 tsp. pure vanilla extract
- 1/2 tsp. lime or lemon extract
- 1/4 cup key lime juice

INSTRUCTIONS

1. **Do not preheat the oven.** Grease and flour a bundt cake pan.
2. Cream butter and sugar until light and fluffy (3-4 minutes with an electric mixer on medium speed).
3. In a separate bowl, combine flour, baking powder, and baking soda.
4. Add cream cheese to the butter-sugar mixture and beat until smooth.
5. Gradually add eggs, one at a time, beating well after each addition. Stir in vanilla, lime or lemon extract, and key lime juice.
6. Gradually add the dry ingredients to the batter, mixing on low speed until just combined.
7. Pour batter into the prepared pan.
8. Place in a cold oven, set to 325°F, and bake for 1 hour 15 minutes or until a toothpick comes out clean.
9. Cool in the pan for 10 minutes, then transfer to a wire rack.
10. Optionally, drizzle with a key lime juice and powdered sugar glaze.
11. Slice and serve.

Note: This cake can be stored in an airtight container at room temperature for several days. For longer storage, refrigerate the cake.

Red Velvet
Pound Cake - Scratch

INGREDIENTS

- 2 1/2 cups all-purpose flour
- 2 cups granulated sugar
- 1 tsp. baking soda
- 1 tsp. cocoa powder
- 1 tsp. salt
- 1 cup buttermilk
- 1 1/2 cups vegetable oil
- 2 large eggs
- 2 Tbsp. red food coloring
- 1 tsp. white vinegar
- 1 tsp. vanilla extract

INSTRUCTIONS

1. Preheat the oven to 325°F.
2. In a large mixing bowl, combine the all-purpose flour, granulated sugar, baking soda, cocoa powder, and salt. Mix well.
3. In a separate bowl, whisk together the buttermilk, vegetable oil, eggs, red food coloring, white vinegar, and vanilla extract until well combined.
4. Gradually add the wet ingredients to the dry ingredients, mixing until the batter is smooth and well incorporated.
5. Grease and flour two 9-inch round cake pans. Divide the batter evenly between the prepared cake pans.
6. Bake in the preheated oven for approximately 25-30 minutes, or until a toothpick inserted into the center of the cakes comes out clean.
7. Remove the cakes from the oven and let them cool in the pans for about 10 minutes. Then transfer them to a wire rack to cool completely.
8. Once the cakes have cooled, frost with cream cheese frosting recipe.

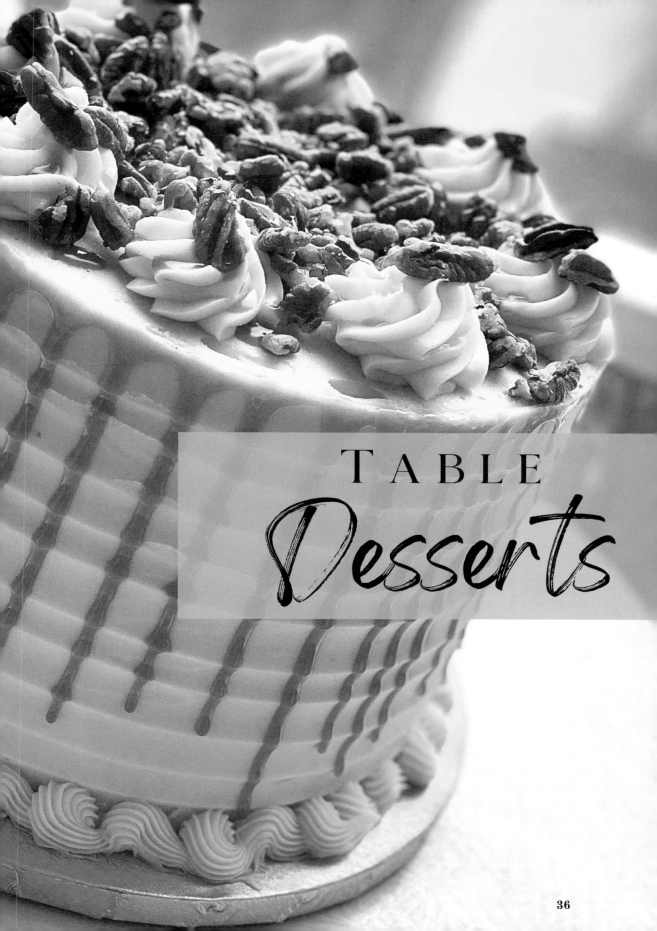

TABLE
Desserts

RICH FOLK
BANANA PUDDING

INGREDIENTS

- 1 box cheesecake pudding
- 1 box banana cream pudding
- (1) 8 oz. pack of cream cheese
- 1 can condensed milk
- 2 cups whole milk
- (1) 8 oz. container of Cool Whip
- 1 Tbsp. vanilla bean paste or vanilla extract
- Tbsp. banana flavor (*optional*)
- 2 bananas sliced
- wafer cookies or Chessmen® cookies (*optional*)

DIRECTIONS

1. Mix pudding mix and milk into a separate bowl.
2. Mix until smooth and allow to chill for 20-30 minutes.
3. In a separate bowl mix cream cheese, condensed milk, and flavoring together. Mix until smooth.

3. Gently fold in cool whip to cream cheese mixture. Do not over mix. It should be smooth and fluffy.
4. Fold the two mixtures of chilled pudding and cream cheese mixture until well incorporated together.
5. Layer the pudding mixture with wafer cookies and top with cookies.

You can also add fresh strawberries or the Liquid Gold Carmel recipe for an added topping.

COUNTRY LEMONADE ICEBOX PIE

- (1) 12 oz. can evaporated milk
- 2 packages of lemon instant pudding mix
- 1 Tbsp. lemon zest
- (2) 8 oz. packages of cream cheese, room temperature
- 1/2 tsp. vanilla extract
- 1/2 tsp. lemon extract
- (1) 12 oz. can lemonade concentrate
- (1) 9-inch graham cracker pie crust + (1) 6-pack mini graham cracker pie crust shells

whipped cream for topping (optional)

INSTRUCTIONS

1. Whisk together milk and pudding mix until mixture has thickened.
2. Beat cream cheese, extracts, and lemon zest until fluffy.
3. Add milk mixture and beat until smooth and creamy.
4. Pour mixture into pie crusts.
5. Cover and chill until firm.
6. Serve chilled and top with whipped cream for presentation.

Scan Here

Milk Chocolate Chip Turtle Brownies

Ingredients

- 2/3 cup all-purpose flour
- 1/4 tsp. baking soda
- 1/2 tsp. sea salt
- 1/2 cup sugar
- 3 Tbsp. unsalted butter
- 2 Tbsp. whole milk
- 2 1/2 cups milk chocolate chips
- 2 large eggs
- 1 tsp. vanilla bean gel or pure vanilla extract

Instructions

1. Preheat your oven to 325°F. Prepare an 8 x 8 square baking pan by spraying the pan and lining with parchment paper and set aside.
2. In a bowl whisk together the flour, baking soda, & salt
3. In a sauce pan add your butter, milk, and sugar and bring to a boil. Remove the pan from heat and add in chocolate chips. Stir until all have been melted and smooth.
4. Add in eggs and vanilla and mix until smooth.
5. Add flour mixture stirring until combined. Spread the batter evenly into pan and sprinkle chocolate chips on top as well before baking.
6. Bake for 25-30 minutes.
7. Top brownies with caramel sauce, pecans, and chocolate ganache drizzle. Cut brownies and enjoy!

Cookie Butter
Banana Pudding

Ingredients

1 box cheesecake pudding
1 box banana cream pudding
1 8 oz. pack of cream cheese
1 can condensed milk
2 cups whole milk
8 oz. container cool whip
1 Tbsp. vanilla bean paste or vanilla extract
1 Tbsp. banana flavor (optional)
Wafer cookies
Biscoff cookies
1 container Biscoff cookie butter
2 bananas, sliced

Instructions

1. Mix pudding mix and milk into a separate bowl. Mix until smooth and allow to chill for 20-30 minutes.
2. In a separate bowl mix cream cheese, condensed milk, and flavoring together. Mix until smooth.
3. Gently fold in cool whip to cream cheese mixture. Do not over mix. It should be smooth and fluffy.
4. Fold the two mixtures of chilled pudding and cream cheese mixture until well incorporated together.
5. Layer the pudding mixture with wafer cookies and top with cookies.

You can also add fresh strawberries or the Liquid Gold Carmel recipe for an added topping.

Brown Butter
Sweet Potato Pie

- 2 - 3 large sweet potatoes
- 1 stick of salted butter, browned
- 12 oz. can evaporated milk
- 1 tsp. vanilla bean paste
- 1 tsp. butter vanilla extract
- 2 tsp. cinnamon
- 1/4 tsp. nutmeg
- 3/4 cup granulated sugar
- 1/4 cup brown sugar
- 1 Tbsp. flour
- 3 eggs, room temperature, slightly beaten
- 2 (9-inch) pie crusts

INSTRUCTIONS

1. Preheat your oven to 350°F.
2. Melt butter in a pan over medium heat. You want to brown the butter until it is fragrant in smell and a beautiful amber color. Set aside to cool.
3. The mixture should be creamy with all strings are removed.
4. In a bowl, add sweet potatoes, browned butter, evaporated milk, spices, sugars, eggs, extracts, and flour.
5. Mix until well combined (if you prefer to taste your mix to ensure the spice level is right, do this before adding the eggs).
6. Pour filling into pie crust
7. Bake for 45-50 minutes.
8. Remove from oven and allow to cool completely.
9. Refrigerate for 2-3 hours and enjoy!

STRAWBERRY & CREAM COOKIES

INGREDIENTS

- 1 cup unsalted butter, room temperature
- 1 cup light brown sugar, packed
- 1/4 cup granulated sugar
- 2 eggs, room temperature
- 1 tsp. vanilla extract
- 2 tsp. strawberry extract
- 2 1/3 cups all-purpose flour
- 3/4 tsp. baking soda
- 1/2 tsp. salt
- 1 cup white chocolate chips
- 1 cup freeze-dried strawberries

INSTRUCTIONS

1. Preheat oven to 350°F and line a baking sheet with parchment paper.
2. In a stand mixer, beat butter, brown sugar, and granulated sugar until light and fluffy.
3. Add eggs and vanilla extract, beat until smooth.
4. Mix in flour, baking soda, and salt until combined.
5. Fold in freeze-dried strawberries and white chocolate chips.
6. Scoop dough onto prepared sheet, spacing 2 inches apart.
7. Bake at 350°F for 12 minutes until edges are golden brown and centers are slightly underdone.
8. Cool on sheet briefly, then transfer to wire rack to cool completely.
9. Enjoy! Makes 14 cookies.

COOKIES & CREAM CHEESECAKE

Set oven to 325°F (may vary depending on your oven)

Crust Instructions

- 2 cups Oreo cookies, finely crushed
- 1/2 cup melted butter
- 2 Tbsp. sugar

Instructions:

1. Melt butter and combine with graham cracker crumbs. Be sure to come up the side of the pan.
2. Bake for 10 minutes in springform pan.

Filling

- (4) 8 oz. packs Philadelphia cream cheese (full fat)
- 1 2/3 cups sugar (2 cups if you like it sweet)
- 1/4 cup cornstarch or flour
- 1/2 cup sour cream
- 4 eggs
- 1 Tbsp. vanilla bean gel
- 3/4 cups heavy cream
- 1 tsp. almond extract
- 1 cup crushed Oreo cookies (will be folded in at the end)

FILLING INSTRUCTIONS

1. Mix cream cheese and sugar until smooth add sour cream, corn starch, and flavoring.
2. Slowly add heavy cream.
3. Add eggs one at a time to incorporate.
4. Remove from mixer and fold in crushed Oreo cookies.
5. Pour mixture into prepared springform pan.
6. Wrap the entire side of pan in foil to allow for even baking.
7. Add pan to a water bath and bake for one hour a twenty minutes. Once the cheesecake you will turn the oven off, crack the oven door and allow the cheesecake to cool in the oven.
8. Once cooled remove it and place in fridge to allow to firm for 6-8 hours.
9. Top with crushed Oreo cookies, drizzle with chocolate ganache.

COOKIE BUTTER CHEESECAKE

Set oven to 325°F (may vary depending on your oven)

Crust Instructions

- 2 cups Biscoff cookies, finely crushed
- 1/2 cup melted butter
- 2 Tbsp. sugar

Instructions:

1. Melt butter and combine with graham cracker crumbs. Be sure to come up the side of the pan.
2. Bake for 10 minutes in springform pan.

Filling

- (4) 8 oz. packs Philadelphia cream cheese (full fat)
- 2 cups sugar
- 1/4 cup cornstarch or flour
- 1/2 cup sour cream
- 4 eggs
- 1 tsp. vanilla extract
- 3/4 cups heavy cream
- 2 tsp. Amaretto liquor

FILLING INSTRUCTIONS

1. Mix cream cheese and sugar until smooth add sour cream, corn starch, and flavoring.
2. Slowly add heavy cream.
3. Add eggs one at a time to incorporate.
4. Remove from mixer and fold in crushed Oreo cookies.
5. Pour mixture into prepared springform pan.
6. Wrap the entire side of pan in foil to allow for even baking.
7. Add pan to a water bath and bake for one hour a twenty minutes. Once the cheesecake you will turn the oven off, crack the oven door and allow the cheesecake to cool in the oven.
8. Once cooled remove it and place in fridge to allow to firm for 6-8 hours.
9. Melt Biscoff cookie butter and prepare for drizzle. Top with crushed cookies and drizzle cookie butter over the top.

VANILLA BEAN CHEESECAKE

Set oven to 325°F (may vary depending on your oven)

Crust Instructions

- 2 cups graham cracker crumbs, finely crushed
- 1/2 cup melted butter
- 2 Tbsp. sugar

Instructions:

1. Melt butter and combine with graham cracker crumbs. Be sure to come up the side of the pan.
2. Bake for 10 minutes in springform pan.

Filling

- (4) 8 oz. packs Philadelphia cream cheese (full fat)
- 2 cups sugar
- 1/4 cup cornstarch
- 1/2 cup sour cream
- 4 eggs
- 1 tsp. vanilla bean gel
- 3/4 cups heavy cream
- 1 tsp. Almond extract

FILLING INSTRUCTIONS

1. Mix cream cheese and sugar until smooth add sour cream, corn starch, and flavoring.
2. Slowly add heavy cream.
3. Add eggs one at a time to incorporate.
4. Remove from mixer and fold in crushed Oreo cookies.
5. Pour mixture into prepared springform pan.
6. Wrap the entire side of pan in foil to allow for even baking.
7. Add pan to a water bath and bake for one hour a twenty minutes. Once the cheesecake you will turn the oven off, crack the oven door and allow the cheesecake to cool in the oven.
8. Once cooled remove it and place in fridge to allow to firm for 6-8 hours.
9. Top with whipped cream and enjoy!

GEORGIA PEACH CROISSANT

INGREDIENTS

2-3 ripe peaches, peeled and diced or canned peaches

1/2 cup granulated sugar

1/2 tsp. ground cinnamon

1 tsp. vanilla extract

4 pre-made croissants or canned

1 tsp. melted butter

INSTRUCTIONS

1. Preheat your oven to 350°F.

2. In a sauce pan, combine the diced peaches, sugar, cinnamon, and vanilla extract. Stir well over medium heat. Let the mixture simmer for about 5-10 minutes on low heat.

3. Slice the pre-made croissants in half horizontally, creating a top and bottom half.

4. Spoon the peach mixture onto the bottom half of each croissant. Be generous with the filling, but avoid overfilling to prevent the croissants from becoming too soggy.

5. Place the top half of each croissant back onto the filled bottom half, creating a sandwich.

6. Brush the melted butter over the tops of the croissants.

7. Optional: sprinkle crushed streusel mixture over the buttered tops of the croissants.

8. Place the peach-filled croissants on a baking sheet lined with parchment paper and bake 10-12 minutes or until golden brown.

9. Remove from the oven and let the Peach Cobbler Croissants cool for a few minutes. Top with vanilla glaze.

Serve warm and enjoy the Georgia Peach Croissants as a delightful dessert or breakfast treat!

PEACH TURNOVER

INGREDIENTS

2 cups diced peaches

Corn Starch Slurry (1 Tbsp. corn starch + 1 Tbsp. water mixed – acts as a thickener)

2 Tbsp. brown sugar

2 Tbsp. white sugar

1 tsp. cinnamon

1 tsp. nutmeg

2-3 Tbsp. unsalted butter

2 puff pastry sheets

1 large egg (for egg wash)

INSTRUCTIONS

1. Pre-heat oven to 350°F.
2. Add butter to a pan on medium heat and melt
3. Add in peach mixture and cook on medium heat until peaches have softened.
4. Lightly dust your work with flour
5. Roll pastry sheet and cut into four equal squares
6. Add a small amount of the peach filing and fold over allowing each corner to meet
7. Using a fork, lightly press down on all edges.
8. Lightly beat the egg and apply to the turnovers using a pastry brush.
9. Cut 3 slits in the middle to allow air to escape while baking
10. Line a baking sheet with parchment paper and bake for 15-20 minutes or until golden brown.
11. Serve with ice cream and top with caramel sauce or enjoy alone!

Peach Cobbler Dump Cake

Ingredients

(2) 29 oz. cans of peaches (one drained)

1/2 cup brown sugar

1/2 cup white sugar

Corn Starch Slurry (1 Tbsp. corn starch + 1 Tbsp. water mixed – acts as a thickener)

1/2 tsp. nutmeg

1/2 tsp. cinnamon

1 box white cake mix

1/2 cup butter

Instructions

1. Pre-heat oven to 325°F.
2. Grease 9x13 pan.
3. Add peaches, sugars, spices, & corn starch slurry to a pan.
4. Spread cake mix over the top of the peaches to completely cover.
5. Pour melted butter over the top of the cake mix.
6. Bake for 45-50 mins or until crust is done and browned.
7. Remove from oven and brush crust with melted cinnamon butter.
8. Enjoy warm with ice cream of your choice!

THE ELITE COOKIE

INGREDIENTS

- 1 cup unsalted butter, softened but not melted
- 3/4 cup light brown sugar packed
- 3/4 cup granulated sugar
- 2 1/4 cups all-purpose flour spooned into the cup then leveled
- 1/2 tsp. salt
- 2 large eggs, room temperature
- 2 tsp. vanilla extract
- 1 tsp. baking soda
- 2 cups chocolate, chopped or chocolate chips

NOTES

1. Use room temperature eggs for less spreading
2. No need to chill your dough
3. For chewy chocolate chip cookies: add 2 extra ounces (1/4 cup) of flour, 2 extra egg yolks, and replace all the white sugar with brown sugar.
4. For cakey chocolate chip cookies: add 2 extra ounces (1/4 cup) of flour and replace the baking soda with an equal amount of baking powder.
5. For crispy chocolate chip cookies: use melted butter, increase the white sugar by 4 ounces (1/2 cup) and decrease the brown sugar by 4 oz. (1/2 cup).

INSTRUCTIONS

1. Preheat your oven to 375°F and line two large cookie sheets with parchment paper (not wax paper).
2. Add softened butter to the bowl of your stand mixer with the whisk attachment and cream until smooth.
3. Add in the brown sugar and white sugar and whisk on low until light and fluffy (about 2 minutes).
4. Add eggs one at a time, letting each mix in fully before adding the next.
5. Add vanilla, salt, and baking soda.
6. Add flour and chocolate chips and mix until just combined.
7. Scoop onto your cookie sheet using a #20 cookie scoop or about two Tablespoons of dough per cookie.
8. Bake for 6 minutes, rotate the pan then bake for another 5-6 minutes or until the center is no longer shiny. **Do not over-bake.**
9. Cookies will be soft at first but will harden as they cool.

OLD FASHIONED
PEANUT BUTTER CHEWS

INGREDIENTS

- 2 cups peanut butter
- 2 cups of sugar
- 2 cups light corn syrup
- 10 cups of cereal
- 1 Tbsp. vanilla extract
- 1 pinch of salt

INSTRUCTIONS

1. Grease a sheet pan.
2. Over low heat, melt peanut butter, sugar, and corn syrup in a pot
3. Once the peanut mixture has melted, remove from heat and pour over cereal. Combined until mixed.
4. Pour mixture onto a greased sheet pan.
5. Allow to cool and cut into squares.
   Optional: Drizzle with milk chocolate or white chocolate.

GLAZES
Frostings
& FILLINGS

CHOCOLATE DREAM
FROSTING

INGREDIENTS

- 2 sticks unsalted butter, room temperature
- 3 cups powdered sugar
- 1/2 cup Hershey's Special Dark cocoa powder
- 2 Tbsp. vanilla extract
- 1 tsp. Almond Extract
- 6-8 Tbsp. whole milk

INSTRUCTIONS

1. In a large mixing bowl, add the room temperature unsalted butter.
2. Use a hand mixer or stand mixer to beat the butter until it becomes creamy and smooth.
3. Gradually add the powdered sugar to the bowl, about 1 cup at a time. Beat the mixture on low speed after each addition until the sugar is fully incorporated.
4. Add the cocoa powder to the bowl. Mix it in with the butter and sugar mixture until well combined.
5. Add the vanilla extract and almond extract to the bowl. Mix well until all the ingredients are fully incorporated.
6. Gradually add the whole milk to the bowl, 1 tablespoon at a time. Beat the mixture on medium speed until it reaches a smooth and spreadable consistency. If needed, add more milk, 1 tablespoon at a time, until you achieve the desired consistency.
7. Continue to beat the frosting for an additional 1-2 minutes to make it light and fluffy.

Your delicious Frosting is now ready to be used as a frosting for cakes, cupcakes, or any other dessert.

Simple Syrup

INGREDIENTS

- 1 cup granulated sugar
- 1 cup water
- Optional: Flavorings such as vanilla extract, citrus zest, or flavored liqueur

INSTRUCTIONS

1. In a small saucepan, combine the granulated sugar and water.
2. Place the saucepan over medium heat and stir the mixture until the sugar has completely dissolved.
3. Once the sugar has dissolved, bring the mixture to a gentle boil.
4. Reduce the heat to low and let the syrup simmer for about 5 minutes, stirring occasionally.
5. After 5 minutes, remove the saucepan from the heat and let the syrup cool slightly.
6. If desired, stir in your preferred flavorings such as vanilla extract, citrus zest, or flavored liqueur. This step is optional but can add extra flavor to the syrup.
7. Let the simple syrup cool completely before using.

TO USE ON CAKES

1. Once your cake has cooled, use a pastry brush to lightly brush the simple syrup onto the cake layers. This will help keep the cake moist and add a touch of sweetness.
2. You can also use a spray bottle to evenly distribute the simple syrup over the cake layers if preferred.
3. If you're making a layered cake, repeat the process of brushing or spraying the simple syrup on each layer.
4. Note: The amount of simple syrup used may vary depending on the size and number of cake layers. Adjust the recipe accordingly.
5. Enjoy your moist and flavorful cake with the help of this simple syrup recipe!

CARAMEL SAUCE

INGREDIENTS

- 1 cup sugar
- 6 Tbsp. salted butter
- 1/2 cup heavy cream (room temperature)
- 1 Tbsp. vanilla extract or vanilla bean paste
- Pinch of sea salt

INSTRUCTIONS

1. Once your cake has cooled, use a pastry brush to lightly brush the simple syrup onto the cake layers. This will help keep the cake moist and add a touch of sweetness.
2. You can also use a spray bottle to evenly distribute the simple syrup over the cake layers if preferred.
3. If you're making a layered cake, repeat the process of brushing or spraying the simple syrup on each layer.
4. Note: The amount of simple syrup used may vary depending on the size and number of cake layers. Adjust the recipe accordingly.

Enjoy the rich and indulgent caramel sauce on your favorite desserts or use it as a topping for ice cream, pancakes, or other treats.

STREUSEL TOPPING

INGREDIENTS

- 1 cup all-purpose flour
- 1/2 cup brown sugar
- 1/4 cup granulated sugar
- 1/2 tsp. cinnamon, depending on preference
- 1/4 tsp. kosher salt
- 6 Tbsp. cold butter, diced small

INSTRUCTIONS

1. Preheat oven to 350°F. Line baking sheet with parchment paper.
2. In a small bowl combine the 1 cup flour, 1/2 brown sugar, 1/4 cup granulated sugar, 1/4 -1/2 tsp. cinnamon, and 1/4 tsp salt.
3. Pinch the butter into the mixture with your fingers gently until small clumps are formed no larger than the size of a pea. The texture should be like coarse wet sand with clumps in it.
4. Put it in the freezer for 20 minutes to chill.
5. Spread chilled streusel over any baked good and follow recipe directions for baking.
6. To bake ahead- spread the streusel onto a prepared baking sheet and bake for 10-12 minutes. If there were larger chunks of butter and they melted, that's ok, you'll break it up anyway!
7. Once the streusel has cooled, break up larger clumps and sprinkle over desserts.

BROWN SUGAR GLAZE

INGREDIENTS

- 1/2 cup unsalted butter
- 1 cup brown sugar
- 1/2 cup evaporated milk
- 2 cups powdered sugar
- 1 tsp. vanilla extract

INSTRUCTIONS

1. In a saucepan, melt the unsalted butter over medium heat.
2. Add the brown sugar to the melted butter and stir until the sugar has dissolved.
3. Slowly pour in the evaporated milk while stirring continuously.
4. Bring the mixture to a gentle boil and let it simmer for about 2 minutes, stirring occasionally.
5. Remove the saucepan from heat and let it cool for a few minutes.
6. Gradually whisk in the powdered sugar until the glaze is smooth and well combined.
7. Stir in the vanilla extract and mix well.

Your brown sugar glaze is now ready to use!
Drizzle it over your favorite baked goods or desserts.

Brown Butter Sweet Potato Pie Filling

INGREDIENTS

- 2-3 large sweet potatoes
- 1 stick of salted butter, browned
- 12 oz. can evaporated milk
- 1 tsp. vanilla bean paste
- 1 tsp. butter vanilla extract
- 2 tsp. cinnamon
- 1/4 tsp. nutmeg
- 3/4 cup granulated sugar
- 1/4 cup brown sugar
- 1 Tbsp. flour
- 3 eggs, room temperature, slightly beaten

INSTRUCTIONS

1. Preheat your oven to 350°F.
2. Melt butter in a pan over medium heat. You want to brown the butter until it is fragrant in smell and a beautiful amber color. Set aside to cool.
3. Puree cooked sweet potatoes in a blender until smooth. This method will ensure the mixture is creamy and all strings are removed.
4. In a bowl, add sweet potatoes, browned butter, evaporated milk, spices, sugars, eggs, extracts, and flour.
5. Mix until well combined. If you prefer to taste your mix to ensure the spice is right, do this before adding the eggs.
6. Pour filling into an oven-safe dish
7. Bake for 45-50 minutes.
8. Remove from oven and allow to cool completely.
9. Refrigerate filling until ready to use. You can pour chilled filling into a piping bag and use as a filling for various pies, cakes and treats.

CARAMEL
BUTTERCREAM

INGREDIENTS

- 4 sticks unsalted butter
- 6-8 cups confectioners' sugar, sifted
- 2-3 Tbsp. heavy whipping cream (add more until you reach the desired consistency)
- 1 Tbsp. caramel extract
- 1 tsp. pure vanilla extract

INSTRUCTIONS

1. In a large mixing bowl, add the unsalted butter. Make sure the butter is at room temperature for easier mixing.
2. Use a hand mixer or stand mixer to beat the butter until it becomes creamy and smooth.
3. Gradually add the sifted confectioner's sugar to the bowl, about 1 cup at a time. Beat the mixture on low speed after each addition until the sugar is fully incorporated.
4. Add the heavy whipping cream, starting with 2 tablespoons. Beat the mixture on medium speed until it reaches a smooth and spreadable consistency. If needed, add more cream, 1 tablespoon at a time, until you achieve the desired consistency.
5. Stir in the caramel extract and pure vanilla extract. Mix well until all the ingredients are fully combined.
6. Continue to beat the frosting for an additional 1-2 minutes to make it light and fluffy.

Your delicious Caramel Buttercream is now ready to be used as a frosting for cakes, cupcakes, or any other desserts.

Cinnamon Cream Cheese

INGREDIENTS

- 4 sticks unsalted butter
- 6-8 cups powder sugar
- 1/4 cup heavy whipping cream
- 6 tsp. cinnamon & sugar
- 2 Tbsp. vanilla extract

INSTRUCTIONS

1. In a large mixing bowl, add the unsalted butter. Make sure the butter is at room temperature for easier mixing.
2. Using a hand mixer or stand mixer, beat the butter on medium speed until it becomes creamy and smooth.
3. Gradually add the powdered sugar to the butter, about 1 cup at a time. Beat on low speed after each addition until the sugar is fully incorporated.
4. Pour in the heavy whipping cream and continue to beat the mixture on medium speed until it reaches a light and fluffy consistency.
5. In a separate small bowl, combine the cinnamon and sugar. Mix well.
6. Add the cinnamon and sugar mixture to the frosting and beat on low speed until it is fully incorporated.
7. Finally, add the vanilla to the mixture and beat for an additional 1-2 minutes until everything is well combined.

Your Cinnamon Cream Cheese Frosting is now ready to be used as a delicious topping for cakes, cupcakes, or any other desserts.

CLASSIC BUTTERCREAM

INGREDIENTS

- 4 sticks unsalted butter
- 6-8 cups confectioner's sugar, sifted
- 1 cup shortening
- 2-3 Tbsp. heavy whipping cream (add more until you reach the desired consistency)
- 1 Tbsp. pure vanilla flavor
- 1 tsp. almond extract (optional)

INSTRUCTIONS

1. In a large mixing bowl, add the unsalted butter. Make sure the butter is at room temperature for easier mixing.
2. Using a hand mixer or stand mixer, beat the butter on medium speed until it becomes creamy and smooth.
3. Gradually add the sifted confectioner's sugar to the butter, about 1 cup at a time. Beat on low speed after each addition until the sugar is fully incorporated.
4. Add the shortening to the mixture and continue to beat on low speed until it is well combined with the butter and sugar.
5. Pour in the heavy whipping cream, starting with 2 tablespoons. Beat the mixture on medium-high speed for a few minutes until it reaches a light and fluffy consistency. If needed, you can add more heavy whipping cream, 1 tablespoon at a time, until you achieve the desired consistency.
6. Add the pure vanilla flavor and almond extract (if using) to the mixture and beat for an additional 1-2 minutes until everything is well combined.

Your Classic Buttercream is now ready to be used as frosting for cakes, cupcakes, or any other desserts.

CREAM CHEESE BUTTERCREAM

INGREDIENTS

- 4 sticks unsalted butter
- 6-8 cups confectioners' sugar, sifted
- 1 cup shortening
- 2-3 Tbsp. heavy whipping cream (add more until you reach the desired consistency)
- 1 block cream cheese
- 1 Tbsp. pure vanilla flavor
- 1 tsp. almond extract (optional)

INSTRUCTIONS

1. Whip butter & shortening until creamy.
2. Add in sifted powdered sugar one cup at a time.
3. Add in flavoring as desired

Double recipe for average cake recipe.

CHANTILLY CREAM

INGREDIENTS

- 16 oz. tub Marsapone cheese
- 8 oz. cream cheese
- 1 tsp. vanilla extract
- 1 lemon
- 2 cups heavy cream
- 1 cup powdered sugar

INSTRUCTIONS

1. Chill icing bowl.
2. Combine Marscapone cheese, cream cheese, and vanilla.
3. Zest 1 lemon into mix, squeeze 1/2 of the lemon.
4. Mix heavy cream in cold mixing bowl until it forms stiff peaks.
5. Add powdered sugar to heavy cream and mix well.
6. Fold all ingredients together

Coconut Filling

INGREDIENTS

- 1/2 cup brown sugar
- 1/2 cup granulated sugar
- 3 egg yolks
- 1 stick butter
- 1 cup evaporated milk
- 1 cup chopped pecans
- 1 cup shredded coconut
- 1 tsp. vanilla extract

INSTRUCTIONS

1. Cook all wet ingredients on medium heat while whisking.
2. Once the mixture begins to bubble, remove from heat and add pecans and coconut.
3. Finally, add the vanilla extract.
4. Allow to chill and thicken.

Allow to chill after cooking.

CLASSIC VANILLA GLAZE

INGREDIENTS

- 1 cup powdered sugar
- 1-2 Tbsp. milk
- 1/2 tsp. vanilla extract or vanilla bean gel

INSTRUCTIONS

1. In a small mixing bowl, sift the powdered sugar to remove any lumps.
2. Gradually add the milk, starting with 1 tablespoon, and stir until the mixture reaches a smooth and pourable consistency. Add more milk if needed.
3. Stir in the vanilla extract until well combined.
4. If desired, you can add a few drops of food coloring to achieve a different color for your glaze.
5. Drizzle the vanilla Icing Glaze over your baked goods using a spoon, whisk, or piping bag.
6. Allow the glaze to set for a few minutes before serving.

For a thicker texture, use more powdered sugar or use less milk.

Homemade Cake Release
(Cake Goop)

INGREDIENTS

- 1/2 cup shortening
- 1/2 cup vegetable oil
- 1/2 cup all-purpose flour
- 1 tsp. pure vanilla extract

INSTRUCTIONS

1. Whisk together the shortening and vegetable oil in a medium bowl until smooth, 2 to 3 minutes.
2. Whisk in the flour until it becomes a smooth paste.
3. When ready to use, spread a thin layer using a pastry brush on the inside of a cake pan before adding the batter and baking.

Store cake release in an airtight container at room temperature for up to 1 month.

CREAMY VANILLA GLAZE

INGREDIENTS

- 1 cup powdered sugar (sifted to remove all lumps)
- 1/4 cup unsalted butter, room temperature
- 1/3 cup sweetened condensed milk
- 2 Tbsp. whole milk`
- 1 tsp. vanilla extract

INSTRUCTIONS

1. In a small mixing bowl, sift the powdered sugar to remove any lumps.
2. Gradually add the milk, starting with 1 tablespoon, and stir until the mixture reaches a smooth and pourable consistency. Add more milk if needed.
3. Stir in the vanilla extract until well combined.
4. If desired, you can add a few drops of food coloring to achieve a different color for your glaze.
5. Drizzle the vanilla Icing Glaze over your baked goods using a spoon, whisk, or piping bag.
6. Allow the glaze to set for a few minutes before serving.
7. For a thicker texture, use more powdered sugar or use less milk.

LEMON GLAZE

INGREDIENTS

- 1 cup confectioners' sugar
- 2-3 Tbsp. freshly squeezed lemon juice
- 1 tsp. lemon zest (optional, for extra lemony flavor)

INSTRUCTIONS

1. In a small mixing bowl, whisk together the confectioners' sugar and freshly squeezed lemon juice until smooth and well combined. Adjust the amount of lemon juice to achieve your desired consistency - a thicker glaze will require less liquid, while a thinner glaze will need more.
2. Add in the lemon zest for an extra punch of fresh lemon flavor, if desired. Stir well to incorporate the zest into the glaze.
3. Once your pound cake is baked and slightly cooled, place it on a wire rack set over a baking sheet to catch any drips.
4. Slowly pour the lemon glaze over the top of the pound cake, allowing it to cascade down the sides. Use a spoon or spatula to help spread the glaze evenly, if needed.
5. Let the glaze set for a few minutes before slicing and serving your delicious lemon-glazed pound cake. Enjoy the zesty and sweet combination of flavors in every bite!

This lemon glaze is the perfect finishing touch for your pound cake, adding a bright and refreshing twist that complements the rich and buttery cake beautifully.

CHEESECAKE FILLING

INGREDIENTS

- 1 block cream cheese
- 1 large egg
- 1/3 cup white sugar
- 1 tsp. vanilla extract

INSTRUCTIONS

1. In a mixing bowl, add the cream cheese and use a hand mixer or stand mixer to beat it until it becomes smooth and creamy.
2. Add the large egg to the cream cheese and continue to beat until the egg is fully incorporated.
3. Gradually add the white sugar to the mixture while beating on low speed. Continue to beat until the sugar is well combined and the mixture becomes smooth.
4. Add the vanilla extract to the mixture and beat for an additional 1-2 minutes until everything is evenly mixed.

Your Cheesecake Filling is now ready to be used! You can swirl it into brownie mix or use it in various cake recipes.

STRAWBERRY GLAZE

INGREDIENTS

- 1 cup fresh strawberries
- 1/2 cup granulated sugar
- 2 Tbsp. water
- 1 Tbsp. cornstarch
- 1 tsp. vanilla flavoring

INSTRUCTIONS

1. In a saucepan, combine the chopped strawberries, granulated sugar, and water. Cook over medium heat, stirring occasionally, until the strawberries start to break down and release their juices.
2. In a small bowl, mix the cornstarch with a little water to create a slurry. Add the cornstarch slurry to the strawberry mixture and continue to cook, stirring constantly, until the mixture thickens and becomes glossy.
3. Remove the strawberry glaze from the heat and let it cool slightly. If you prefer a smoother glaze, you can blend it with an immersion blender or regular blender until smooth.
4. Once your pound cake is baked and slightly cooled, pour the strawberry glaze over the top of the cake, allowing it to drip down the sides. Use a spoon or spatula to help spread the glaze evenly if needed.
5. Allow the glaze to set for a few minutes before slicing and serving your delicious strawberry-glazed pound cake. Enjoy the sweet and tangy flavor of the strawberries paired with the moist and rich pound cake.

This strawberry glaze is a vibrant and fresh addition to your pound cake, providing a burst of fruity goodness that will delight your taste buds with every bite.

FRESH STRAWBERRY FILLING

INGREDIENTS

- 2 cups fresh strawberries, hulled and chopped
- 1/4 cup granulated sugar
- 1 Tbsp. cornstarch
- 1 Tbsp. lemon juice
- 1 tsp. pure vanilla flavor

INSTRUCTIONS

1. In a medium saucepan, combine the chopped strawberries, granulated sugar, cornstarch, and lemon juice.
2. Place the saucepan over medium heat and stir the mixture gently until the sugar has dissolved.
3. Continue to cook the mixture, stirring occasionally, until the strawberries release their juices and the mixture thickens, about 5-7 minutes.
4. Remove the saucepan from heat and let the strawberry filling cool completely.

Once cooled, you can use the strawberry filling as a topping for cakes, cupcakes, pies, or as a filling for pastries or crepes.

OLD FASHIONED CARAMEL FROSTING

INGREDIENTS

- 1 stick of butter
- 1/2 cup light brown sugar
- 1/2 cup white sugar
- 1/2 cup heavy cream (add additional tablespoons until desired consistency is reached.)
- 2 cups powdered sugar sifted
- 1 tsp. vanilla extract
- 1 tsp. vanilla bean gel
- 1 pinch of sea salt

INSTRUCTIONS

1. Place the butter white sugar and brown sugar in a medium pot.
2. Stir over medium heat and cook until it comes to a boil (it should look grainy).
3. Add the milk, stir, and bring the mixture back to a boil (the brown sugar should now magically dissolve!).
4. Remove the pan from the heat, and add the powdered sugar and vanilla.
5. Beat with a wooden spoon until smooth. Use the hot icing immediately to frost any cake, otherwise, it will start to set.
6. If the icing stiffens and becomes unusable, just put the pan back on medium heat and stir until it melts again.
7. Let the icing cool and set once on the cake – it should look smooth and beautiful!

CHEESECAKE DESSERT SHOOTERS FILLING

INGREDIENTS

- 8 oz. cream cheese, softened
- 1/2 cup powdered sugar
- 1 tsp. vanilla extract
- 1/2 cup heavy cream

INSTRUCTIONS

1. In a medium-sized bowl, beat the softened cream cheese until smooth and creamy.
2. Add the powdered sugar and vanilla extract to the bowl and continue to beat until well combined and fluffy.
3. In a separate bowl, whip the heavy cream until stiff peaks form.
4. Gently fold the whipped cream into the cream cheese mixture until fully incorporated.
5. Transfer the cheesecake filling to a piping bag or a zip-top bag with one corner snipped off for easy filling.
6. Fill dessert shooter glasses or small cups with the cheesecake filling, layering it with your choice of crushed cookies, fruit compote, or other desired toppings.
7. Refrigerate the dessert shooters for at least 1 hour before serving to allow the filling to set.

Now you have a creamy and delicious cheesecake filling that is perfect for dessert shooters! Enjoy!

APPLE PIE FILLING

INGREDIENTS

- 5-6 medium-sized apples, peeled, cored, and thinly sliced
- 1/2 cup granulated sugar
- 1/4 cup brown sugar
- 2 Tbsp. all-purpose flour
- 1 tsp. ground cinnamon
- 1/4 tsp. ground nutmeg
- 1/4 tsp. ground cinnamon
- 1/4 tsp. all spice
- 1/4 tsp. salt
- 1 tablespoon lemon juice
- 4 tablespoon unsalted butter

INSTRUCTIONS

1. In a large bowl, combine the sliced apples, granulated sugar, brown sugar, flour, spices, and lemon juice. Toss well to coat the apples evenly.
2. Let the apple mixture sit for about 15-20 minutes to allow the flavors to meld together.
3. In a large skillet, melt the butter over medium heat. Add the apple mixture to the skillet and cook for about 5-7 minutes, stirring occasionally, until the apples soften slightly and the mixture thickens.
4. Remove the skillet from the heat and let the apple pie filling cool completely before using it in a pie crust or any other dessert recipe.

Now you have a delicious homemade apple pie filling ready to be used in your favorite apple desserts!

PEACH FILLING

INGREDIENTS

- 4 cups fresh peaches, peeled and diced or (1- 29 oz. can of peaches) recommended
- 4 Tbsp. unsalted butter
- 1/2 cup granulated sugar
- 2 Tbsp. cornstarch
- 1/2 tsp. lemon juice
- 1/2 tsp. vanilla extract or (1 Tbsp. vanilla bean gel) recommended
- 1/4 tsp. ground cinnamon
- 1/4 tsp. all spice
- 1/4 tsp. nutmeg

INSTRUCTIONS

1. In a medium saucepan, combine the diced peaches, sugar, cornstarch, lemon juice, vanilla extract, and all spices. Stir well to combine.
2. Place the saucepan over medium heat and cook the mixture, stirring frequently, until the peaches are softened and the mixture thickens – about 8-10 minutes.
3. Remove the saucepan from the heat and let the peach filling cool completely.
4. Once cooled, use the peach filling as a delicious filling for pies, tarts, cakes, or pastries.

Enjoy your homemade peach filling!

CORE
Recipes
&
VARIATIONS

No Fail Chocolate Cake

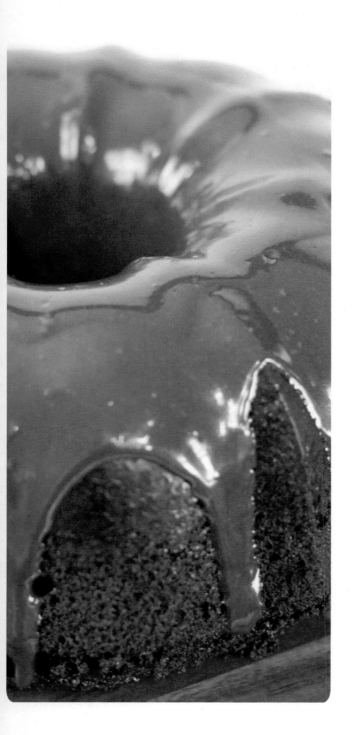

INGREDIENTS

1 box chocolate cake mix
1 cup all-purpose flour
1 cup sugar
1/2 cup oil
1/2 cup buttermilk
1 cup hot black coffee
3 eggs
1 Tbsp. pure vanilla flavor
1 Tbsp. cocoa powder

INSTRUCTIONS

1. Preheat your oven to 325°F.
2. Whisk all dry ingredients together.
3. Add wet ingredients.
4. Bake until toothpick comes out clean.

Pineapple Coconut Rum Cake

INGREDIENTS

3 whole eggs
1 cups water
1/2 cup buttermilk
1/2 cup vegetable oil
1 tsp. coconut extract
1 tsp. rum extract
1 tsp. vanilla bean paste or pure vanilla flavor
1 cup sugar
1 cups sifted all-purpose flour
1 box pineapple cake mix
1 box pineapple gelatin mix
1 cup shredded coconut flakes

INSTRUCTIONS

1. Preheat oven to 325°F.
2. Grease desired pans depending on dessert you are making. This recipe works well for layers, sheets, & cupcakes.
3. Add all wet ingredients to mixing bowl.
4. Add all dry ingredients.
5. Mix until well combined all lumps are out.
6. Add batter to pan.
7. Bake 40-50 minutes or until tooth pick comes out clean.

CARAMEL DREAM CAKE

INGREDIENTS

1 box yellow cake mix
1 cups all-purpose flour
1 cup sugar
1/2 cup oil
1 cup buttermilk
1/2 cup water
3 eggs
1 Tbsp. vanilla bean flavor
1 Tbsp. caramel flavor

INSTRUCTIONS

1. Preheat your oven to 325°F.
2. In a large mixing bowl, combine all ingredients. Mix well until all the ingredients are thoroughly combined and the batter is smooth.
3. Grease desired pans with cooking spray or butter, making sure to coat the entire surface of the pan.
4. Pour the cake batter into the prepared bundt cake pan, spreading it evenly. Swirl in caramel sauce into batter
5. Bake in the preheated oven for about 40-45 minutes, or until a toothpick inserted into the center of the cake comes out clean.
6. Remove the cake from the oven and let it cool in the pan for about 10 minutes. Then, carefully invert the pan onto a wire rack to release the cake. Let the cake cool completely.

Sprinkle Me
Cake

INGREDIENTS

1 box white cake mix
1 cup all-purpose flour
1 cup sugar
1/2 cup oil
1 cup buttermilk
1/2 cup water
3 eggs
1 Tbsp. vanilla bean flavor
1 tsp. almond extract
1/2 cup rainbow sprinkles

INSTRUCTIONS

1. Preheat your oven to 325°F.
2. In a large mixing bowl, combine all ingredients. Mix well until all the ingredients are thoroughly combined and the batter is smooth.
3. Grease a bundt pan or cake pan with cooking spray or butter, making sure to coat the entire surface of the pan.
4. Fold Sprinkles into batter. Pour the cake batter into the prepared bundt cake pan, spreading it evenly.
5. Bake in the preheated oven for about 40-45 minutes, or until a toothpick inserted into the center of the cake comes out clean.
6. Remove the cake from the oven and let it cool in the pan for about 10 minutes. Then, carefully invert the pan onto a wire rack to release the cake. Let the cake cool completely.

Butter Pecan Cake

INGREDIENTS

1 box yellow cake mix
1 cup all-purpose flour
1 cup sugar
1/2 cup oil
1 cup buttermilk
1/2 cup water
3 eggs
1 Tbsp. vanilla bean flavor
1 tsp. butter flavor
1/2 cup chopped pecans

INSTRUCTIONS

1. Preheat your oven to 325°F.
2. In a large mixing bowl, combine all ingredients. Mix well until all the ingredients are thoroughly combined and the batter is smooth.
3. Grease desired pans with cooking spray or butter, making sure to coat the entire surface of the pan.
4. Bake in the preheated oven for about 40-45 minutes (layer & sheet cakes), or until a toothpick inserted into the center of the cake comes out clean.
5. This recipe can be used for sheet cakes, layer cakes, & cupcakes.

KEY LIME CAKE

INGREDIENTS

1 box lemon cake mix
1 box lime gelatin mix
1 cup all-purpose flour
1 cup sugar
1/2 cup oil
1 cup buttermilk
1/2 cup water
3 eggs
2 Tbsp. key lime juice
1 Tbsp. lemon extract

INSTRUCTIONS

1. Preheat your oven to 325°F.
2. In a large mixing bowl, combine all ingredients. Mix well until all the ingredients are thoroughly combined and the batter is smooth.
3. Grease desired pans with cooking spray or butter, making sure to coat the entire surface of the pan.
4. Pour the cake batter into the prepared bundt cake pan, spreading it evenly.
5. Bake in the preheated oven for about 40-45 minutes, or until a toothpick inserted into the center of the cake comes out clean.
6. Remove the cake from the oven and let it cool in the pan for about 10 minutes. Then, carefully invert the pan onto a wire rack to release the cake. Let the cake cool completely.

No Fail Vanilla Cake

INGREDIENTS

1 box white cake mix
1 cups all-purpose flour
1 cup sugar
1 box white chocolate or
vanilla pudding mix
1/2 cup oil
1 cup buttermilk
1/2 cup water
3 eggs
1 Tbsp. vanilla bean flavor
1 tsp. almond

INSTRUCTIONS

1. Preheat your oven to 325°F.
2. In a large mixing bowl, combine all ingredients. Mix well until all the ingredients are thoroughly combined and the batter is smooth.
3. Grease desired pans with cooking spray or butter, making sure to coat the entire surface of the pan.
4. Pour the cake batter into the prepared bundt cake pan, spreading it evenly.
5. Bake in the preheated oven for about 40-45 minutes, or until a toothpick inserted into the center of the cake comes out clean.
6. Remove the cake from the oven and let it cool in the pan for about 10 minutes. Then, carefully invert the pan onto a wire rack to release the cake. Let the cake cool completely.

Old Fashioned Coconut Cake

Ingredients

2-3/4 cups all-purpose flour
2- 1/2 tsp. baking powder
1/2 tsp. salt
1 cup unsalted butter, softened
2 cups granulated sugar
4 large eggs
1 tsp. vanilla extract
1 cup coconut milk
1-1/2 cups sweetened shredded coconut

For the Frosting

1 cup unsalted butter, softened
4 cups powdered sugar
1/4 cup coconut milk
1 tsp. vanilla extract
1-1/2 cups sweetened shredded coconut, for topping

Instructions

1. Preheat your oven to 325°F. Grease and flour (3) 8-inch round cake pans.
2. In a medium bowl, whisk together the flour, baking powder, and salt. Set aside.
3. In a large bowl, cream together the butter and sugar until light and fluffy. Add the eggs, one at a time, beating well after each addition. Add the vanilla extract.
4. Gradually add the flour mixture to the butter mixture, alternating with the coconut milk. Begin and end with the flour mixture. Mix until just combined. Fold in the shredded coconut.
5. Divide the batter evenly among the prepared cake pans. Smooth the tops with a spatula.
6. Bake for 25-30 minutes, or until a toothpick inserted into the center of the cakes comes out clean.
7. Remove the cakes from the oven and let them cool in the pans for 10 minutes. Then, transfer the cakes to a wire rack to cool completely.
8. In the meantime, prepare the frosting. In a mixing bowl, beat the softened butter until creamy. Gradually add the powdered sugar, coconut milk, and vanilla extract. Beat until smooth and fluffy.
9. Once the cakes have cooled, frost the top of 1 cake layer. Place the second layer on top and frost it. Finally, place the third layer on top and frost the entire cake, including the sides.
10. Sprinkle shredded coconut over the top and sides of the cake, pressing gently to adhere. Refrigerate the cake for at least 1 hour before serving.

Chocolate Dream Cake Doctored Version

INGREDIENTS

1 box chocolate cake mix
1 cups all-purpose flour
3/4 cup cocoa powder
1 box chocolate gelatin mix
1 cup sugar
1/2 cup oil
1 cup fresh strong brewed black coffee
1/2 cup buttermilk
3 eggs
1 Tbsp. vanilla bean flavor
1 tsp. almond extract

INSTRUCTIONS

1. Preheat your oven to 325°F.
2. In a large mixing bowl, combine all ingredients. Mix well until all the ingredients are thoroughly combined and the batter is smooth.
3. Grease desired pans with cooking spray or butter, making sure to coat the entire surface of the pan.
4. Pour the cake batter into the prepared bundt cake pan, spreading it evenly.
5. Bake in the preheated oven for about 40-45 minutes, or until a toothpick inserted into the center of the cake comes out clean.
6. Remove the cake from the oven and let it cool in the pan for about 10 minutes. Then, carefully invert the pan onto a wire rack to release the cake. Let the cake cool completely.

CHOCOLATE DREAM CAKE
SCRATCH VERSION

INGREDIENTS

1-3/4 cups all-purpose flour
3/4 cup Hershey's cocoa powder or high quality baking powder
2 cups granulated sugar
1-1/2 tsp. baking powder
1-1/2 tsp. baking soda
1 tsp. salt
1 cup milk
1/2 cup vegetable oil
2 large eggs
2 tsp. pure vanilla extract
1 tsp. almond extract
1 cup fresh strong brewed black coffee

INSTRUCTIONS

1. Preheat your oven to 325°F and prepare (2) 8" cake pans or Bundt cake pan.
2. In a large bowl sift together your flour and cocoa powder, add in your baking powder and soda, along with the salt and sugar. Mix well.
3. Create a well in the center and add in your milk, oil, eggs, and extract. Mix well for 2 minutes to combine. Once combined pour in your hot coffee, mix together until fully incorporated.
4. Pour into 2 parchment paper lined 8" cake pans. Bake for 30-35 minutes until fully baked.

RUBY RED VELVET CAKE

INGREDIENTS

1 box red velvet cake mix
1 cup all-purpose flour
1 cup granulated sugar
1/2 cup vegetable oil
1/2 cup water
1 cup buttermilk
4 large eggs
1 tsp. vanilla extract

INSTRUCTIONS

1. Preheat your oven to 325°F.
2. In a large mixing bowl, combine all ingredients. Mix well until all the ingredients are thoroughly combined and the batter is smooth.
3. Grease a bundt cake pan with cooking spray or butter, making sure to coat the entire surface of the pan.
4. Pour the cake batter into the prepared bundt or cake pan, spreading it evenly.
5. Bake in the preheated oven for about 40-45 minutes, or until a toothpick inserted into the center of the cake comes out clean.
6. Remove the cake from the oven and let it cool in the pan for about 10 minutes. Then, carefully invert the pan onto a wire rack to release the cake. Let the cake cool completely.

COUNTRY LEMONADE CAKE

INGREDIENTS

1 box lemon cake mix
1 cups all-purpose flour
1 cup sugar
1/2 cup oil
1 cup buttermilk
1/2 cup water
3 eggs
1 tsp. vanilla bean flavor
2 tsp. pure lemon flavor
1 lemon, squeezed
lemon zest of 1 lemon

INSTRUCTIONS

1. Preheat your oven to 325°F.
2. In a large mixing bowl, combine all ingredients. Mix well until all the ingredients are thoroughly combined and the batter is smooth.
3. Grease a bundt pan or cake pan with cooking spray or butter, making sure to coat the entire surface of the pan.
4. Pour the cake batter into the prepared bundt cake pan, spreading it evenly.
5. Bake in the preheated oven for about 40-45 minutes, or until a toothpick inserted into the center of the cake comes out clean.
6. Remove the cake from the oven and let it cool in the pan for about 10 minutes. Then, carefully invert the pan onto a wire rack to release the cake. Let the cake cool completely.

VERY BERRY STRAWBERRY CAKE

INGREDIENTS

1 box strawberry cake mix
1 cups all-purpose flour
1 cup sugar
1/2 cup oil
1/2 cup buttermilk
1 cup water
3 eggs
2 tsp strawberry extract
1/2 box strawberry gelatin
mix

INSTRUCTIONS

1. Preheat your oven to 325°F.
2. In a large mixing bowl, combine all ingredients. Mix well until all the ingredients are thoroughly combined and the batter is smooth.
3. Grease desired pans with cooking spray or butter, making sure to coat the entire surface of the pan.
4. Bake in the preheated oven for about 40-45 minutes (layer & sheet cakes), or until a toothpick inserted into the center of the cake comes out clean.
5. This recipe can be used for sheet cakes, layer cakes, & cupcakes.

WHITE ALMOND CAKE

INGREDIENTS

1 box white cake mix
1 cup all-purpose flour
1 cup sugar
1/2 cup oil
1/2 cup buttermilk
1 cup water
4 egg whites
1 Tbsp. almond extract or
almond emulsion
1 tsp. vanilla bean paste

INSTRUCTIONS

1. Preheat your oven to 325°F.
2. In a large mixing bowl, combine all ingredients. Mix well until all the ingredients are thoroughly combined and the batter is smooth.
3. Grease desired pans with cooking spray or butter, making sure to coat the entire surface of the pan.
4. Bake in the preheated oven for about 40-45 minutes (layer & sheet cakes), or until a toothpick inserted into the center of the cake comes out clean.
5. This recipe can be used for sheet cakes, layer cakes, & cupcakes.

COCKTAILS & MOCKTAILS

DeDe's Peach Sweet Tea

INGREDIENTS

- 6 cups boiling hot water
- 4 black tea bags
- 2-3 ripe peaches

SIMPLE SYRUP INGREDIENTS

- 1 cup water
- 2 cups sugar

INSTRUCTIONS

1. In a large heatproof pitcher or container, add 6 cups of boiling hot water.
2. Place 4 black tea bags into the hot water and let them steep for about 5 minutes. You can adjust the steeping time based on your preference for tea strength.
3. While the tea is steeping, prepare the peaches. Wash and slice 2-3 ripe peaches. You can leave the skin on for added flavor and texture.
4. In a separate saucepan, combine peaches, 1 cup of water, and 2 cups of sugar to make the simple syrup. Heat the mixture over medium heat, stirring constantly until the sugar is completely dissolved. This will take about 5 minutes. Once the sugar is dissolved, remove the saucepan from heat and let the simple syrup cool.
5. Strain peaches from simple syrup.
6. After the tea has steeped, remove the tea bags and discard them.
7. Add the sliced peaches to the pitcher or container with the tea.
8. Pour the cooled simple syrup into the pitcher or container with the tea and peaches. Stir well to combine all the ingredients.
9. Place the pitcher or container in the refrigerator and let it chill for at least 2 hours, or until it's cold and the flavors have melded together
10. Before serving, give the Peach Sweet Tea a good stir to distribute the peach flavor evenly. You can also add ice cubes to individual glasses for a refreshing cold drink.

Pour the Peach Sweet Tea into glasses, garnish with a peach slice or mint leaves if desired, and enjoy!

STRAWBERRY PINEAPPLE MOSCATO

INGREDIENTS

- 1 cup strawberries, hulled and sliced
- 1 cup pineapple chunks
- 1 bottle of Moscato wine
- 1/4 cup pineapple juice
- 1/4 cup strawberry syrup or simple syrup
- Fresh mint leaves (for garnish)
- Ice cubes

INSTRUCTIONS

1. In a blender, combine the strawberries, pineapple chunks, pineapple juice, and strawberry syrup. Blend until smooth.
2. Strain the mixture through a fine-mesh sieve to remove any seeds or pulp.
3. In a pitcher, combine the strained fruit mixture with the Moscato wine. Stir well to combine.
4. Refrigerate the mixture for at least 1 hour to chill.
5. Fill glasses with ice cubes and pour the Strawberry Pineapple Moscato mixture over the ice.
6. Garnish each glass with fresh mint leaves.

Serve and enjoy your refreshing Strawberry Pineapple Moscato cocktail!

BOURBON BERRY SMASH

INGREDIENTS

- 2 oz. bourbon
- 3/4 oz. fresh lemon juice
- 1/2 oz. simple syrup
- 1/4 cup fresh raspberries
- Lemon wedge or cherry, for garnish (optional)
- Ice cubes

INSTRUCTIONS

1. In a cocktail shaker, muddle the raspberries and combine the bourbon, lemon juice, and simple syrup.
2. Fill the shaker with ice cubes and shake vigorously for about 15 seconds.
3. Strain the mixture into an on-the-rocks glass filled with ice.
4. Garnish with a lemon wedge or cherry, if desired.

Enjoy your Bourbon Berry Smash!

Remember, you can always adjust the quantities of the ingredients to suit your taste preferences.

Cheers!

MANGO PUNCH MOJITO

INGREDIENTS

- 2 oz. white rum
- 1/2 cup fresh mango chunks
- 10 fresh mint leaves
- 1 oz. lime juice
- 1 Tbsp. sugar or simple syrup
- Splash of club soda
- Ice cubes
- Lime wedges and mint sprigs (for garnish)

INSTRUCTIONS

1. In a cocktail shaker, muddle the fresh mango chunks and mint leaves together until they are well crushed.
2. Add the white rum, lime juice, and sugar (or simple syrup) to the shaker.
3. Fill the shaker with ice cubes and shake well to combine all the ingredients.
4. Strain the mixture into a glass filled with ice cubes.
5. Top off the glass with club soda for a refreshing fizz.
6. Garnish with a lime wedge and a sprig of mint.

Stir gently and enjoy your tropical Mango Punch Mojito!

Hennessy Lemon Drop

INGREDIENTS

- 1.5 oz. of Hennessy V.S Cognac
- 1 oz. of freshly squeezed lemon juice
- 0.75 oz. of simple syrup
- Lemon wedge, for garnish

INSTRUCTIONS

1. Fill a cocktail shaker with ice.
2. Add 1.5 ounces of Hennessy V.S.O.P. Cognac to the shaker.
3. Pour in 1 ounce of freshly squeezed lemon juice.
4. Add 0.75 ounce of simple syrup to the shaker.
5. Shake the mixture vigorously for about 10-15 seconds to chill the ingredients.
6. Strain the cocktail into a chilled martini glass.
7. Garnish the drink with a lemon wedge on the rim of the glass.

Serve and enjoy your refreshing Hennessy Lemon Drop!

FRONT PORCH
HENNESSY SWEET TEA

INGREDIENTS

- 2 oz. Hennessy Cognac
- 4 oz. sweet tea (premade or homemade)
- 1/2 oz. lemon juice
- Lemon wedges (for garnish)
- Ice cubes

INSTRUCTIONS

1. In a glass filled with ice cubes, pour 2 oz of Hennessy Cognac.
2. Add 4 ounces of sweet tea to the glass.
3. Squeeze in 1/2 ounce of lemon juice for a touch of acidity.
4. Stir the mixture gently to combine the flavors.
5. Garnish with a lemon wedge on the rim of the glass.
6. Serve and enjoy your refreshing Hennessy Sweet Tea!

This cocktail combines the smoothness of Hennessy Cognac with the sweetness of tea and a hint of lemon. It's a delightful and unique twist on the classic sweet tea.

Cheers!

TYE RITA
PINEAPPLE MARGARITA

INGREDIENTS

- 2 oz. tequila
- 1 oz. triple sec
- 2 oz. pineapple juice
- 1 oz. freshly squeezed lime juice
- 1 oz. simple syrup
- Pineapple wedge or lime wedge (for garnish)
- Salt (for rimming the glass)

INSTRUCTIONS

1. Rim a margarita glass with salt. To do this, rub a lime wedge around the rim of the glass, then dip the rim into a plate of salt.
2. Fill a cocktail shaker with ice.
3. Add tequila, triple sec, pineapple juice, lime juice, and simple syrup to the shaker.
4. Shake well to combine and chill the ingredients.
5. Fill the prepared margarita glass with ice.
6. Strain the cocktail mixture into the glass.
7. Garnish with a pineapple wedge or lime wedge.
8. Serve and enjoy your delightful Pineapple Margarita!

This tropical twist on the classic margarita is perfect for enjoying on a sunny day or at any fiesta.

Cheers!

POPPING PEACH
PROSECCO MARGARITA

INGREDIENTS

- 2 oz tequila
- 2 oz peach puree (see below)
- 1 oz orange liqueur - can sub for peach schnapps to really amp up the peach factor!
- 1/2 oz lime juice
- 1/2 oz agave
- Prosecco to taste

INSTRUCTIONS

PEACH PUREE

Combine 1 cup peaches, peeled and 1/2 cup water in blender. Blend until smooth.

1. Combine tequila, peach puree, orange liqueur, lime juice, and agave in a cocktail shaker.
2. Add ice and shake until chilled.
3. Strain into a glass filled with ice.
4. Top with Prosecco and a peach slice.

You may also use the peaches from
Dede's Peach Sweet Tea

Strawberry Pineapple Lemonade (Mocktail)

INGREDIENTS

- 1 cup strawberries, sliced
- 1 cup pineapple chunks
- 1/2 cup freshly squeezed lemon juice
- 2-3 cups sugar (adjust to taste)
- 4 cups cold water
- Ice cubes
- Fresh mint leaves (optional, for garnish)

INSTRUCTIONS

1. Rim a margarita glass with salt. To do this, rub a lime wedge around the rim of the glass, then dip the rim into a plate of salt.
2. Fill a cocktail shaker with ice.
3. Add tequila, triple sec, pineapple juice, lime juice, and simple syrup to the shaker.
4. Shake well to combine and chill the ingredients.
5. Fill the prepared margarita glass with ice.
6. Strain the cocktail mixture into the glass.
7. Garnish with a pineapple wedge or lime wedge.
8. Serve and enjoy your delightful Pineapple Margarita!

This tropical twist on the classic margarita is perfect for enjoying on a sunny day or at any fiesta.

Cheers!

You may also use the peaches from
DeDe's Peach Sweet Tea

Index

Index

Index

Credits

Author
Jeromie Jones

Photography
Jeromie Jones,
Monique Millender Photography,
Sarai Mena Maldonado

Food Styling
Jeromie Jones

Editors
Jeromie Jones, Cerissa Jordan

Design & Layout
Jeromie Jones, WriteUp Services, Inc.

Publisher
WriteUp Services, Inc.